To

_____

From:

_____

Date:

_____

Fill In the Blank

With life changing scriptures

Volume 1

Novell Phillips

Fill In The Blank with life- changing scriptures Volume 1

All Scripture quotations are from the
King James Version of the Holy Bible.

Publisher: Novell Phillips

Printed in the United States of America

ISBN:978-0-615-94165-3

CONTENTS

Introduction

Fill In The Blank with life changing scriptures is a devotion hand book that I have written to encourage the people of GOD. To execute the power of GOD's word. Death and life are in the power of the tongue. For out of the abundance of the heart the mouth speaketh. Jesus said it is the spirit that quickened; the flesh profited nothing: the words that I speak unto you, they are spirit, and they are life. I believe that the people of GOD should say the same .Over the years as I begin to learn God's word. I recognize that certain scriptures I would quote concerning my own personal problems would change I would fill my own name in the blank. Low and behold my fears would disappear ,my troubles would go away.

Fill In The Blank

The eyes of my understanding was being enlightened. I begin

to comprehend the word of GOD.I shared this revelation with

others and GOD moved by his Spirit on their behalf also.

As it is written for the word of GOD is quick, and powerful,

and sharper than any two-edged sword, piercing even to

the dividing asunder of soul and spirit, and of the

joints and marrow, and is a discerner of the thoughts

and intents of the heart. I understand now that

GOD is not a man. Numbers 23:19 GOD is a spirit.

John 4:24 and the word is spirit. John 6:63 and

the word is GOD. Ephesians 6:17 most of all

GOD is love. 1 John 4:8.

All scripture is given by inspiration of God, and is

profitable for doctrine, for reproof, for correction

for instruction in righteousness. **2 Timothy 3:16 .**

So then faith cometh by hearing, and hearing by the word

of God. Romans 10:17 .For by thy words thou shalt be

justified, and by thy words thou shalt be condemned

Matthew 12:37. The entrance of thy words giveth light;

it giveth understanding unto the simple . Psalm 119:130

And my speech and my preaching was not with enticing

Words of man's wisdom, but in demonstration of the

Spirit and of power: 1 Corinthians 2:4

The centurion man asked Jesus to "speak the word only and my servant shall be healed". Matthew 8:8 Speak the word to your love ones. Speak the word to your husband .

Speak the word to your wife. Speak the word to your son and to your daughter. Speak the word to your family.

Speak the word to your friends. Speak the word to your associates. Speak the word to your acquaintances, and even to your enemies. Fill their names in the blank .

Send the word to their spirit daily. Psalm 107:20 He sent his word and healed them, and delivered them from their destructions.

Matthew 9:29 According to your faith be it unto you.

GOD said for I will hasten my word to perform it.
Jeremiah 1:12

For Example :

Thy word is a lamp unto ____Denisha____feet, and a light
unto_____Denisha_____path.
Psalm 119:105

Jesus answered and said unto ___Joe_____, Verily, verily, I say unto
__Joe_____, except a man be born again, he cannot see
the kingdom of God.
John 3:3

____Pam_____seek ye the LORD while he may be found, call ye
upon him while he is near.
Isaiah 55:6

In the beginning was the Word, and the Word was with

God, and the Word was God. The same was in the

beginning with God. All things were made by him; and

without him was not anything made that was made. In

him was life; and the life was the light of men. And the

light shineth in darkness; and the darkness comprehended

it not. And the word was made flesh,(Jesus) and dwelt

among us, and we beheld his glory, the glory as of the only

begotten of the Father, full of grace and truth

John 1 :1;2;3;4;5;14

Endorsement
By
Chief Apostle Leonard Lucas, Jr.

This book is an indispensable devotion tool.

It is for anyone who believe in the Word of God.

In its approach the application can truly be a life

rewarding experience. The exceptional work done by Sister

Novell is one of the most

profound principle practiced .I admonish you as you plunge

Into the scripture to open your heart, mind and soul and let

inner transformation be manifested. The Apostle Paul says

that " For the earnest expectation of the creature waited for

the manifestation of the sons of God" (Roman 8:19).

As the Chief Apostle, I encourage you to allow the

Spirit of God to move in your life and in the life of others

as you Fill In The Blanks with life changing scriptures.

Chief Apostle Leonard Lucas, Jr.

Dedication

I Sister Novell dedicate this book to the memorial of my

father Alexander Charles Allen 0f Thibodaux Louisiana

My mother Sallie Phillips Allen of Madison ,

Mississippi and to my daughter Takeisha Dionne Phillips

of Jeanerette ,Louisiana. In whom I will always love

and miss. And to all of my family on my mother's side,

and all of my family on my father's side. To all of my

Church family, friends, associates and acquaintances.

Special Thanks

I want to first give special thanks to God Almighty and
to his Son Jesus Christ for His love and His kindness
and for His Holy Spirit that inspired me to write this
book. I give special thanks to my sisters Jewel L .
Smith ,Linda L. Smith, and Brenda D. Smith for
their moral and financial support. I give special thanks to

my spiritual leaders Chief Apostle Leonard Lucas Jr.
and his wife Prophetess Varanise Lucas for their love,
inspiration and support.

Need Salvation

Fill In The Blank

But what saith it? The word is nigh _____

even in _____mouth, and in

_____heart: that is, the word of faith,

which we preach; That if _____ shalt

confess with _____mouth the

Lord Jesus, and shalt believe in _____

heart that God hath raised him (Jesus) from the dead,

_____ shalt be saved .For with the
heart man believeth unto righteousness; and with the
mouth confession is made unto salvation. For the
scripture saith, Whosoever believeth on him
shall not be ashamed. For whosoever shall call upon

the name of the Lord shall be saved.
Romans 10:8; 9; 10;11;13

15

Fill In The Blank

Verily verily, I say unto _____,except a

man be born again, he cannot see the kingdom of GOD.

John 3:3

Marvel not that I Said unto _____,

_____ must be born again

John 3:7

Fill In The Blank

_____ neither is there salvation in
any other: for there is none other name under heaven given
among men, whereby we must be saved.
Acts 4:12

Plead _____cause, O LORD, with

them that strive with _____: fight

against them that fight against _____.
Take hold of shield and buckler, and stand up for

_____ help. Draw out also the spear
and stop the way against them that persecute

_____:say unto

_____soul, I am thy salvation.
Psalm 35:1;2;3

With long life will I satisty _____and

shew _____my salvation.

Psalms 91:16

Look unto me, _____and be ye
saved all the ends of the earth: for I am GOD, and there is
none else.
Isaiah 45:22

Fill In the Blank

Make haste, O God, to deliver _____ ;

make haste to help _____ ,O LORD.

Let them be ashamed and confounded that seek after

_____ soul: let them be turned

backward, and put to confusion, that desire

_____ hurt. Let them be

turned back for a reward of their shame that say, Aha, aha.

Let all those that seek thee rejoice and be glad in thee:

and let such as love thy salvation say continually,

Let God be magnified. But _____

am poor and needy: make haste unto _____

O God: thou art _____ help and

_____ deliverer; O LORD,
make no tarrying.

Psalm 70: 1;2;3;4;5

Above all, taking the

shield of faith, wherewith

_____ shall be

able to quench all the fiery

darts of the wicked. An take

the helmet of salvation,

and the sword of the Spirit,

which is the word of God.

Ephesians 6:16; 17

Decree Riches

Fill In The Blank

For _____ know the grace of our

Lord Jesus Christ, that, though he was rich, yet for

_____ sakes he became poor,

That _____ through his poverty

Charge _____ that are rich in this world,

that _____ be not highminded, nor
trust in uncertain riches, but in the living God, who giveth

_____ richly all things to enjoy.

That _____ do good ,that

_____ be rich in good works, ready

to distribute, willing to communicate;
1 Timothy 6:17

But my God shall supply all _____ '

need according to his riches in glory by Christ Jesus.
Philippians 4:19

_____ the blessing of the
LORD, it maketh rich, and he addeth no sorrow with it.
Proverbs 10:22

Fill In The Blank

For this cause I bow my knees unto the Father

of our Lord Jesus Christ, Of whom the whole family in

heaven and earth is named. That he would grant

_____, according to the

riches of his glory, to be strengthened with might by his

Spirit in the inner man; That Christ may dwell in

_____ hearts by faith; that

_____, being rooted and grounded

in love, May be able to comprehend with all saints what is

the breadth, and length, and depth, and height; And to

know the love of Christ, which passeth knowledge, that

_____might be filled with

all the fulness of God.
Ephesians 3:14 to 19

Call upon GOD

Fill In The Blank

Then shall _____ call upon me, and

_____ shall go and pray unto me,

and I will hearken unto _____ . And

_____ shall seek me, and find me ,

when _____ shall search

for me with all _____ heart.
Jeremiah 29:12; 13

call unto me ,and I (GOD) will answer thee, and shew

_____ great and mighty things,

which _____ knowest not.

Jeremiah 33:3

Fill In The Blank

_____ shall call upon me, and I will

answer _____: I will be with

_____in trouble;

I will deliver _____, and honour

_____.

Psalms 91:15

_____ The LORD is nigh unto
all them that call upon him, to all that call upon him in truth.
Psalms 145:18

_____ seek ye the LORD

while He may be found, call ye upon him while he is near:
Isaiah 55 :6

And it shall come to pass, that before _____

Call, I will answer; and while _____ are
Yet speaking, I will hear.

Isaiah 65:24

TRUST IN THE LORD

Fill In The Blank

_____Trust in the LORD with

all thine heart; and lean not unto thine own understanding.

In all thy ways acknowledge him, and he shall direct thy

paths. Proverbs 3:5;6

O taste and see _____ that the LORD

is good: blessed is the man that trusteth in him.
Psalms 34:8
Thou wilt keep _____in perfect

peace, _____mind is stayed on

thee: because _____ trusteth in thee.
Isaiah 26:3

In GOD have _____ put_____

trust: _____ will not be afraid what man

can do unto _____.
Psalm 56:11

In GOD _____will praise his word,

In GOD _____ have put

_____ trust _____

Will not fear what flesh can do unto _____
Psalm 56:4

See The Vision

Fill In The Blank

_____Where there is no vision,

the people perish: but he that k eepeth the law, happy is he.
Proverbs 29:18

_____for the vision is yet
for an appointed time, but at the end it shall speak,
and not lie: though it tarry, wait for it; because it will surely
come, it will not tarry. Behold, his soul which is lifted up is
not upright in him: but the just shall live by his faith.
Habakkuk   2; 3; 4

For God speaketh once, yea twice, yet

_____ Perceiveth it not. In a

dream, in a vision of the night, when deep sleep falleth

upon _____, in slumbering upon the

bed; then he openeth the ears of _____,

and sealeth _____ instruction.
Job 33:14;15;16

Special prayers

Fill In The Blank

For this cause we also, since the day we heard it, do not

Cease to pray for _____, and to

desire that _____ might be filled
with the knowledge of his will in all wisdom and spiritual

understanding; That _____ might
walk worthy of the LORD unto all pleasing, being fruitful
In every good work, and increasing in the knowledge of
GOD; Strengthened with all might, according to his glorious
power, unto all patience and longsuffering with joyfulness;
Giving thanks unto the Father, which hath made

_____ meet to be partakers

of the inheritance of the saints in light: Who hath delivered

_____ from the power of

darkness, and hath translated _____

Into the kingdom of his dear Son:
Colossians 1:9;10;11;12;13

Fill In The Blank

Wherefore I also, after I heard of _____

faith in the Lord Jesus, and love unto all the saints,

Cease not to give thanks for _____,

making mention of _____ in my prayers;
That the God of our Lord Jesus Christ, the Father of glory,

may give unto _____ the spirit of wisdom
and revelation in the knowledge of him: The eyes of

_____ understanding being

enlightened; that _____ may know

what is the hope of _____ calling, and

what the riches of the glory of _____
inheritance in the saints, And what is the exceeding

greatness of his power to us-ward who believe, according
to the working of his mighty power, Which he wrought in

Christ, when he raised him from the dead, and set him
at his own right hand in the heavenly places, Far above
all principality, and power, and might, and dominion, and

every name that is named, not only in this world, but also
in that which is to come: And hath put all things under his

feet, and gave him to be the head over all things to the

church, Which is his body, the fulness of him that filleth

all in all.
Ephesians 1:18 ;19;20;21;22;23

32

Speak LORD;

for thy Servant heareth

Fill In The Blank

_____ will hear what GOD the LORD

will speak:

for he will speak peace unto his people,

an to his saints: but let_____ not

turn again to folly.
Psalm 85:8

34

Teach

Fill In The Blank

Shew _____

thy ways, O LORD ; Teach

_____thy paths.

Lead_____

in thy truth, and teach_____:

for thou art the GOD of _____

salvation; on thee do _____

wait all the day.
Psalms 25:4;5

36

Fill In The Blank

I will instruct_____ and teach

_____ in the way which

_____ shalt go I will guide

_____with mine eye.
Psalm 32:8

Thus saith the Lord,_____

Redeemer, the Holy One of Israel; I am the Lord

_____God which teacheth

_____ to profit, which leadeth

_____ by the way that

_____ shouldest go.
Isaiah 48: 17

Hearken

Fill In The Blank

And it shall come to pass, if _____

shalt hearken diligently unto the voice of the LORD

_____ God, to observe and to do

all his commandments which I command

_____ this day, that the LORD

_____ God will set

_____ on high above

all nations of the earth:
Deutronomy 28:1

And all these blessings shall come on

_____, and overtake

_____, if

_____

shalt hearken unto the voice of the LORD

_____ God.
Deuteronomy 28:2   :

39

The Word

Fill In The Blank

_____for the word of God is quick,

and powerful, and sharper than any twoedged sword,

piercing even to the dividing asunder of soul and spirit,

and of the joints and marrow, and is a discerner of the

thoughts and intents of the heart .
Hebrews 4:12
_____prevented the dawning
of the morning, and cried: I hoped in thy word.
Psalm 119: 147

Thy word have _____hid in

_____ heart, that

_____might not sin against thee.

Psalm 119:11   The entrance of the words giveth

_____ light; it giveth understanding

Unto the simple Psalm 119:130

Thy word is a lamp unto _____feet,

and a light unto _____ path.

Psalm 119:105

In God will _____praise his word:

in the LORD will _____Praise his word.

Psalm 56:10   Jesus said sanctify _____
through thy truth: thy word is truth .
John 17:17

Choose Life And Live

Fill In The Blank

Deal bountifully with thy servant , _____

that _____may live, and keep

thy word.
Psalm   119:17

_____ shall not die, but live,

and declare the works of the Lord.
Psalm 118 : 17

I call heaven and earth to record this day against

_____ , that I have set before

_____ life and death, blessing

and cursing: therefore choose life, that both _____

and _____ seed may live :

Deuteronomy 30:19

Friend

Fill In The Blank

Henceforth I call _____ not

servants ; for the servant knoweth not what his lord doeth:

but I have called _____ friends; for
all things that I have heard of my Father I have made known

unto _____.
John 15:15

_____ a man that hath friends

must shew himself friendly: and there is a friend that sticketh
closer than a brother.
 Proverbs 18:2 4

Draw Nigh To GOD

Don't Draw Back

Fill In The Blank

_____draw nigh to God,

and he will draw nigh to you.
James 4: 8

_____ now the just shall live

by faith: but if any man draw back, my soul shall have no
pleasure in him.
Hebrews 10:38

Ask GOD

Fill In The Blank

If _____ abide in me, and my words

abide in _____,

_____ shall ask what

_____ will, and it shall

be done unto _____.
John 15:7

Ask and it shall be given _____;seek,

and _____shall find; knock, and

it shall be opened unto _____.
Matthew 7:7

Preach The Word

Fill In The Blank

The Spirit of the Lord is upon _____,

because he hath anointed _____

to preach the gospel to the poor; he hath sent

_____ to heal the

brokenhearted, to preach deliverance to the captives, and

recovering of sight to the blind, to set at liberty them that are

bruised. To preach the acceptable year of the Lord.

Luke 4:18;19

And _____ went forth, and preached

every where, the Lord working with _____
and confirming the word with signs following. A-men'
Mark 16:20

Peace

Fill In The Blank

For I know the thoughts that I think toward

_____, saith the   Lord,

thoughts of peace, and not of evil, to give

_____ an expected end.
Jeremiah 29;11

Great peace have _____

which love thy law: and nothing shall offend

_____.

Psalm 119:165

_____ when a man's ways

please the Lord he maketh even his enemies to be at peace
with him.
Proverbs 16: 7

Thou wilt keep_____in

Perfect peace, _____mind

Is stayed on thee; because _____
Trusteth in thee.
Isaiah 26;3

Fear

Fill In The Blank

Have not I commanded thee? Be strong and of a good courage; be not afraid, neither be thou dismayed: for the

LORD _____ God is with

_____ whithersoever

_____ goest .
Joshua 1:9

_____the fear of the LORD is
the beginning of wisdom: a good understanding have all
they that do his commandments: his praise endureth for ever.
Psalm 111:10

And _____ fear not them which kill the
body, but are not able to kill the soul: but rather fear him
(God) which is able to destroy both soul and body in hell.
Matthew 10:28

_____There is no
fear in love; but perfect love casteth out fear: because
fear hath torment. He that fearth is not made perfect in
love.
1 John 4:18

O fear the LORD ,_____ his saints:
for there is no want to them that fear him.
Psalm 34:9

Fill In The Blank

The LORD is _____ shepherd;

_____ shall not want. He maketh

_____ to lie down in green pastures:

he leadeth _____ beside the still water

he restoreth _____ soul: he leadeth

_____ in the paths of righteousness
for his name's sake. Yea though _____
walk through the valley of the shadow of death,
_____ will fear no evil: for thou art

with _____ ; thy rod and thy staff they

comfort _____ .Thou preparest

a table before _____ in the presence

of _____ enemies: thou anointest

_____ head with oil;

_____ cup runneth over.
Surely goodness and mercy shall follow
_____ all the days of

_____ life: and

_____ will dwell in the house of the
Lord for ever.
Psalm 23:1;2;3;4;5;6

Fill In the Blank

In righteousness shalt _____ be

established: _____ shalt be far from

oppression; for _____ shalt not fear:
and from terror; for it shall not come near

_____. Behold, they shall surely
gather together, but not by me: Whosoever shall gather

together against _____ shall fall

for _____ sake. No weapon that

is formed against _____ shall prosper;

and every tongue that shall rise against

_____

in judgment thou shalt condemn. This is the heritage of the

servants of the LORD, and _____
righteousness is of me, saith the LORD.
Isaiah 54; 14;15;17

Fill In The Blank

_____be not afraid of

sudden fear,neither of the desolation of the wicked, when
it cometh.

For the LORD shall be _____

confidence, and shall keep

_____ foot from being taken.

Proverbs 3:25; 26

For GOD hath not given _____

the spirit of fear; but of power, and of love, and of a sound mind.

2 Timothy 1:7

Come, ye children, hearken unto me: I will

teach _____the fear of the Lord .
Psalm 34:11

But _____whoso hearkeneth unto me

(GOD) shall dwell safely, and shall be quiet from fear
of evil.
Proverbs 1: 33

Fill In The Blank

Fear thou not; _____ for I am

with thee: be not dismayed: _____

for I am thy God: I will strengthen _____; yea,

I will help _____; yea, I will uphold

_____ with the right hand of my righteousness.

Behold, all they that were incensed against

_____ shall be ashamed and
confounded: they shall be as nothing; and they that

strive with _____ shall perish.

_____ shalt seek them, and shalt not

find them, even them that contended with _____

they that war against _____ shall be as
nothing, and as a thing of nought. For I the LORD

_____ GOD will hold

_____ right hand, saying unto

_____, Fear not; I will help thee.
Isaiah 41:10;11;12;13

59

Fill In The Blank

_____be not afraid of sudden fear,

neither of the desolation of the wicked, when it cometh.

For the LORD shall be _____

confidence, and shall keep _____

foot from being taken.
Proverbs 3:25; 26

_____sought the Lord ,and he heard

_____, and delivered

_____ from all _____

fears.
Psalm 34:4

HEALING And HEALTH

Fill In The Blank

Heal _____ O LORD, and

_____ shall be healed ;

save_____, and

_____ shall be saved : for

thou art _____ praise.
Jeremiah 17: 14

But he (Jesus) was wounded for_____
transgressions , he(Jesus) was bruised for

_____ iniquities: the chastisement of

_____ peace was upon him ;(Jesus)

and with his stripes _____are healed.
Isaiah 53 :5

62

_____ be not wise
in thine own eyes: fear the LORD, and depart from evil.
It shall be health to

_____navel,
and marrow to

_____ bones.

Proverbs 3:7;8

_____ confess your faults one
to another, and pray one for another, that ye may be healed.
The effectual fervent prayer of a righteous man availeth much.
James 5:16

_____ my son, attend to my words;

Incline thine ear unto my sayings.
_____

let them not depart from thine eyes;
_____

keep them in the midst of thine heart. For they are life unto
those that find them, and health to all their flesh.

_____keep thy heart with all
diligence; for out of it are the issues of life.
Proverbs 4:20;21;22;23;

STAND

Fill In The Blank

Finally, _____ my
brethren, be strong in the Lord, and in the power of his might.

_____ put on the
whole armour of God,

that _____ may be able
to stand against the wiles of the devil. For we wrestle not
against flesh and blood, but against principalities, against
powers, against the rulers of the darkness of this world,
against spiritual wickedness in high places. Wherefore take
unto _____ the whole

Armour of God, that _____
may be able to withstand in the evil day, and having done all,

to stand Stand therefore having _____
loins girt about with truth, and having on the breastplate of

righteousness;and _____ feet
shod with the preparation of the gospel of peace;
Ephesians 6:10;11;12;;13;14;15

65

Fill In The Blank

There shall not any man be able to stand before

_____ all the

days of _____ life:
as I (GOD) was with Moses, so I (GOD)will be with

_____ : I will not fail

_____, nor forsake

_____.

Joshua 1:5

Stand fast therefore in the liberty wherewith Christ hath

made_____ free, and be not
entangled again with the yoke of bondage.
Galatians 5:1

Humble

Fill In The Blank

_____Thou art

snared with the words of thy mouth, thou art taken with

the words of thy mouth. Do this now, my son, and deliver

thyself,when thou art come into the hand of thy friend; go,

humble thyself, and make sure thy friend.
Proverbs 6:2 ;3

_____ humble

 yourselves in the sight of the LORD, and he shall lift you up.
James 4: 10

_____ humble yourselves
therefore under the mighty hand of God, that he may exalt

you in due time: Casting All_____

 care upon him; for he careth for _____.
1 Peter 5:6;7

Sleep

Fill In The Blank

_____will lift up

_____

eyes unto the hills, from whence cometh

_____ help.

_____help cometh
from the LORD , which made heaven and earth. He

will not suffer _____ foot to be

moved: he that keepeth _____
will not slumber . Behold, he that keepeth Isreal
shall neither slumber nor sleep .
Psalm 121:1;2;3;4

When _____liest down,

_____ shalt not be afraid:

yea, _____shalt lie down, and

_____sleep shall be sweet.
Proverbs 3:24

Fill In The Blank

_____ love not sleep,

lest _____ come to poverty;

open _____ eyes, and

_____ shalt be satisfied
with bread.
Proverbs 20:13

_____yet a little sleep,
a little slumber, a little folding of the hands to sleep:

so shall _____poverty come

as one that travelleth, and _____
want as an armed man.
Proverbs 6:10;11

Order Steps

Fill In The Blank

Order _____ steps in thy word:
and let not any iniquity have dominion over

_____.

Psalm 119:133

The steps of a good man are ordered by the LORD: and

he delighteth in _____ way.

Though _____fall,

_____shall not be utterly
cast down:

For the LORD upholdeth_____
With his hand.
Psalm 37:23;24

73

GOD Pleasure

Fill In The Blank

For it is God which worketh in

_____

both to will and to do of his good pleasure.
Philippians 2:13

Let them shout for joy, and be glad, that favour

_____

righteous cause: yea, let them say continually,
Let the LORD be

magnified, which hath pleasure in the prosperity of

his servant_____.
Psalms35:27

75

HAND

Fill In the Blank

And _____

called on the God of Israel, saying, Oh that thou wouldest

bless_____ indeed, and enlarge

_____ coast, and that

thine hand might be with _____,

and that thou wouldest keep _____

from evil, that it may not grieve _____!

and God granted _____ that which

_____requested.
1 Chronicles 4:10

_____ The king's heart is in
the hand of the LORD, as the rivers of water: he turneth it
whithersoever he will.
Proverbs 21:1

77

Fill In The Blank

The LORD is _____

keeper: the LORD is _____

shade upon _____

right hand. The sun shall not smite

_____

by day, nor the moon by night. The LORD shall preserve

_____from all evil: he shall

preserve _____soul. The LORD shall

preserve _____ going out and

_____ coming in from this time
forth, and even for evermore .
Psalm 121: 5;6;7;8

78

Prosper

Fill In The Blank

Believe in the LORD your God, so shall

_____

be established; believe his prophets, so shall

_____ prosper.
2 Chronicles 20:20

Beloved. I wish above all things that

_____ mayest prosper

and be in health even as _____
soul prospereth. 3 John 1: 2

Only be thou strong and very courageous, that

_____mayest observe to
do according to all the law, which Moses my servant
commanded thee: turn not from it to the right hand or to

the left, that _____mayest

prosper whithersoever _____
goest. Joshua 1:7

Fill In The Blank

This book of the law shall nct depart out of

_____ mouth; but

_____ shalt meditate therein

day and night, that _____

mayest observe to do according to all that is written therein:

for then _____ shalt make

_____ way prosperous, and

then _____shalt have good

success Joshua 1:8

Things

Fill In The Blank

_____Even God ,who
quickeneth the dead, and calleth those things
which be not as though they were.
Romans 4:17

But seek ye first the kingdom of God, and his
righteousness; and al. these things shall be

added unto _____
Matthew 6:33

Charge _____that are rich in this

world, that _____ be not
highminded, nor trust in uncertain riches, but in the living

God, who giveth _____ richly

all things to enjoy; That _____do good,

that _____ be rich in good work,
ready to distribute, willing to communicate;
1 Timothy 6:17;18

The Angels Of The LORD

Fill In The Blank

The angel of the Lord encampeth round about

_____ that fear him ,and

delivered _____.
Psalm 34:7

For he shall give his angels charge over

_____,to keep

_____in all

_____ ways. They shall bear

_____ up in their hands,

Lest _____ dash

_____ foot against a stone.
Psalm 91:11;12

Fill In The Blank

Let them be confounded and put to shame that seek after

_____ soul: let them be turned
back and brought to confusion that devise

_____hurt. Let them be as chaff
before the wind: and let the angel of the LORD chase them.
Let their way be dark and slippery: and let the angel of the
LORD persecute them. For without cause have they hid for

_____ their net in a pit, which without

cause they have digged for _____
soul. Let destruction come upon him at unawares ; and let
his net that he hath hid catch himself: into that very destruction

let him fall. And _____soul shall
be joyful in the LORD: it shall rejoice in his salvation.
Psalm 35:4;5;6;7;8;9

86

Give

Fill In The Blank

Every place that the sole of _____
foot shall tread upon, that have I given unto

_____ ,as I said unto Moses
Joshua 1:3

_____ give to him that asketh thee,
and from him that would borrow of thee turn not thou away.
Matthew 5:42

_____ Heal the sick, cleanse the lepers,
raise the dead, cast out devils: freely ye have received,
freely give. Matthew 10:8

I have shewed _____ all things,

how that so labouring _____ ought
to support the weak, and to remember the words of the
Lord Jesus, how he said It is more blessed to give than to
receive. Acts 20:35

_____ Give, and it shall be
Given unto you; good measure, pressed down, and shaken
Together, and running over, shall men give into your bosom.

For with the same measure that _____

Mete withal it shall be measured to _____
again

88

Desire

_____ delight thyself also in the
LORD; and he shall give thee the desires of thine heart.
Psalms 37:4

_____Hope deferred maketh the
heart sick, but when the desire cometh, it is a tree of life.
Proverbs 13:12

_____ The desire accomplished is
sweet to the soul.
Proverbs 13:19

One thing have _____desired of

the LORD, that will _____ seek after;

that _____ may dwell in the house

of the LORD all the days of _____
life, to behold the beauty of the LORD, and to enquire in his
temple. Psalm 27:4

Special Acknowledgements

My sincere appreciation to Miranda Higgins McGhee
of New Orleans Louisiana my Multimedia, life-changing
coach .
To Velvet M. Knight of New Orleans Louisiana, for editing.

To Kamilah Jackson of Signal Hill California for editing.

To Dr. James W. Proctor of crowley Louisiana, for editing.

And to My cousin Mamie H. Pclk of New Orleans Louisiana.
my editior- in-chief.

Schedule Sister Novell to Speak at your church , organization as a keynote speaker,book signing or for other Speaking engagements .

For more information: Email us at sisternovell@ yahoo.com